REBEL HEART

The Untold Story of Sinead O'Connor

By

Morghan Knight

Table of Contents

Introduction

In the world of music, there are few figures as captivating, fearless, and influential as Sinead O'Connor. With her hauntingly powerful voice, unapologetic demeanor, and unwavering commitment to artistic expression, she emerged as a true iconoclast who defied conventions and shattered expectations. Her journey from a troubled youth in Dublin, Ireland, to international stardom and the controversies that defined her career, has left an indelible mark on the music industry and beyond.

"Rebel Heart: The Untold Story of Sinead O'Connor" embarks on a compelling exploration of this enigmatic artist's life,

offering a glimpse into the heart and soul of a woman who dared to be different. This biography peels back the layers of mystery surrounding Sinead, revealing the triumphs and tribulations that shaped her unique perspective on the world.

From her early struggles in a fractured family, to the moment she stunned the world with her iconic protest on a live television broadcast, Sinead O'Connor's life has been a whirlwind of passion, emotion, and creativity. This book seeks to unravel the complexities of her musical genius, her search for spiritual enlightenment, and her relentless pursuit of authenticity in an industry that often demanded conformity.

Through candid accounts from those who knew her best, as well as a meticulous examination of her discography and public appearances, "Rebel Heart" offers readers an intimate look into the soul of an artist who never shied away from speaking her truth. It delves into her personal struggles with mental health, love, loss, and the unyielding determination that drove her to become an enduring voice for change and empowerment.

Beyond her iconic music, Sinead O'Connor's legacy reverberates through the annals of pop culture, leaving a profound impact on future generations of musicians, activists, and free spirits alike. Her story is one of resilience, passion, and the unbridled pursuit of individuality.

Chapter 1

A Troubled Soul

Sinead O'Connor's life began amidst adversity in the heart of Dublin, Ireland. Raised in a broken family, her early years were marred by poverty, instability, and emotional turmoil. Growing up with four siblings in a cramped and struggling household, Sinead faced the harsh realities of a fractured home, leaving an indelible mark on her young soul.

Her parents' marriage was fraught with conflict, ultimately leading to their separation when she was only eight years old. The absence of a stable familial foundation left Sinead feeling lost and isolated, seeking solace in her own thoughts and dreams. As she coped with her family's disintegration, she found refuge in the solace of music, immersing herself in the powerful emotions expressed by artists she admired.

Religion also played a significant role in shaping Sinead's formative years. Raised in a devoutly Catholic environment, she grappled with the rigid dogmas and constraints of the faith. Her upbringing within a religious community exposed her to a world steeped in tradition, yet she felt an innate rebellious spirit urging her to challenge the status quo.

Throughout her adolescence, Sinead's rebellious nature clashed with the societal norms imposed upon her, leading to clashes with authority figures at school and within her community. Despite her academic potential, she struggled to fit into the confines of a traditional education system that failed to recognize her unorthodox creativity.

As her teenage years unfolded, Sinead grappled with the complexity of her emotions. The pain of her troubled upbringing intertwined with her artistic expression, giving rise to a raw and authentic voice that would later resonate with millions around the globe. It was during this time that she began to explore songwriting and music as an outlet for her feelings, setting the foundation for her remarkable musical journey.

Amidst the turmoil of her personal life, Sinead's passion for music became her beacon of hope. She pursued her dream with unwavering determination, performing at local venues and gaining recognition for her unique voice and emotive performances. These early experiences on stage helped her find a sense of belonging and purpose, a stark contrast to the disarray she experienced within her family and society.

Despite the glimmers of success on the local music scene, the weight of her troubled past continued to haunt Sinead. The scars of her tumultuous childhood manifested in emotional struggles and battles with mental health. Wrestling with depression and anxiety, she sought refuge in her music, using it as a therapeutic outlet to confront her inner demons.

As she approached adulthood, Sinead faced the daunting task of forging her path in a world that often misunderstood and underestimated her. The road to success was anything but smooth, fraught with setbacks and challenges that tested her resilience. Yet, with every obstacle she encountered, Sinead's determination to break free from the chains of her troubled past only grew stronger.

In the midst of her struggles, fate intervened, opening a new chapter in Sinead's life. An opportunity arose that would forever change the course of her musical journey. With the support of a growing fan base and industry professionals who recognized her potential, she embarked on a path that would lead to her breakout debut album, "The Lion and the Cobra."

Through adversity, resilience, and unwavering passion, Sinead O'Connor's journey from a troubled soul to an emerging musical force was underway. The challenges of her past would become the foundation of her artistry, infusing her music with a depth and authenticity that would captivate the world. As the stage was set for her meteoric rise, the world eagerly awaited the emergence of a true rebel with a cause, ready to defy conventions and leave an indelible mark on the music industry.

Chapter 2

The Genesis of a Star

As Sinead O'Connor's undeniable talent and captivating presence began to garner attention on the local music scene, the stage was set for her meteoric rise to stardom. Armed with her hauntingly powerful voice and unyielding determination, she embarked on a journey that would lead to the creation of her debut album, "The Lion and the Cobra," a transformative work that would forever etch her name in musical history.

The genesis of Sinead's stardom can be traced back to her encounters with key industry figures who recognized her potential. One such pivotal moment was her meeting with Irish musician and producer Mike Scott, founder of The Waterboys. Scott was impressed by Sinead's talent and offered her an opportunity to contribute vocals to the song "Haunted" for The Waterboys' album "Fisherman's Blues." This collaboration served as a springboard for her career, gaining her wider recognition within the music community.

Emboldened by the positive response to her collaboration with The Waterboys, Sinead began to focus more intently on her songwriting. Drawing from her personal experiences and emotional struggles, she channeled her inner turmoil into her music, resulting in a powerful and authentic body of work. Her songwriting prowess showcased a level of vulnerability and depth that resonated deeply with listeners, setting her apart from her contemporaries.

It was during this time that Sinead caught the attention of Ensign Records, who quickly recognized her potential as a solo artist. The label offered her a recording contract, providing her with the platform she needed to fully explore her musical vision. With newfound support and creative freedom, Sinead set out to craft an album that would showcase the essence of her artistry.

In the summer of 1987, "The Lion and the Cobra" was released to critical acclaim, introducing the world to the raw power of Sinead O'Connor's voice and the depth of her songwriting. The album's lead single, "*Mandinka*," was a roaring success, garnering significant airplay and solidifying her position as a rising star. Audiences were captivated by the haunting melodies and the emotional intensity conveyed through Sinead's vocals.

"*The Lion and the Cobra*" was a revelation, blending elements of rock, folk, and traditional Irish music with Sinead's distinctive vocals and evocative lyrics. Tracks like "Troy" and "Just Like U Said It Would B" showcased her ability to convey a range of emotions, from raw vulnerability to fierce defiance. The album's success earned Sinead a Grammy nomination for Best Female Rock Vocal Performance, catapulting her into the international spotlight.

As her star ascended, Sinead's unconventional appearance and outspoken nature also garnered significant media attention. She challenged societal norms and gender expectations, opting for a shaved head and rejecting the trappings of traditional femininity. Her unapologetic authenticity became a hallmark of her persona, endearing her to a diverse audience and earning her a reputation as an artist who fearlessly spoke her truth.

With the release of "The Lion and the Cobra," Sinead O'Connor emerged as a force to be reckoned with, not just within the music industry but also as a cultural icon.

Her artistry transcended boundaries, resonating with audiences far beyond her Irish roots. Her music became a beacon of hope and empowerment for those who felt marginalized, as her honest and emotive expressions gave voice to their own struggles and triumphs.

As she basked in the glow of her well-deserved success, Sinead O'Connor remained true to her roots and continued to use her platform to advocate for social and political causes close to her heart. Her unyielding commitment to speaking out against injustice and inequality solidified her position as more than just a music star; she became a symbol of resistance and resilience, inspiring a generation to find their voice and stand up for what they believed in.

"The Lion and the Cobra" marked the beginning of a remarkable journey that would see Sinead O'Connor cement her status as an enduring musical icon. With her debut album, she proved that her talent and authenticity were undeniable, paving the way for a groundbreaking career filled with artistic exploration, boundary-pushing, and an unwavering commitment to staying true to herself. The genesis of a star had occurred, and the world eagerly awaited the next chapter in the captivating tale of Sinead O'Connor.

Chapter 3

The Protest Heard Around the World

As Sinead O'Connor's career soared to new heights following the success of "The Lion and the Cobra," the world was about to witness a defining moment that would forever alter the trajectory of her life and legacy. It was on October 3, 1992, during her appearance on NBC's "Saturday Night Live," that Sinead would make a protest heard around the world, shaking the very foundations of the music industry and sparking a fierce debate on religion, feminism, and the power of artistic expression.

As the spotlight focused on Sinead on that fateful evening, the audience braced for another soul-stirring performance. But instead of singing, she stood silent for a few moments, holding a photograph of Pope John Paul II. Then, with a fierce determination in her eyes, she proceeded to tear the photograph into pieces, leaving the viewers stunned and speechless. It was a bold act of protest against the Catholic Church's history of sexual abuse and its complicity in covering up such atrocities.

The fallout from this act of defiance was swift and far-reaching. The controversy dominated headlines and news broadcasts worldwide, with public opinion sharply divided. Some hailed Sinead as a courageous artist using her platform to speak out against injustice, while others condemned her for what they perceived as a disrespectful and blasphemous act.

The incident also had significant repercussions for Sinead's career. Her actions sparked backlash from many quarters, leading to concert cancellations, radio bans, and a boycott of her music by some fans. Record sales for her subsequent albums suffered, and her relationship with the music industry became strained. Despite the challenges, Sinead remained steadfast, unapologetically defending her protest as a legitimate expression of her beliefs and convictions.

In the wake of the "*Saturday Night Live*" incident, Sinead O'Connor continued to confront the controversies and criticisms head-on. She became an outspoken advocate for victims of abuse and an ardent supporter of women's rights. Her unyielding commitment to speaking her truth, regardless of the consequences, earned her both admiration and disdain.

Beyond the immediate aftermath, the protest on "Saturday Night Live" sparked a broader conversation about the intersection of art, politics, and religion. Sinead's actions opened up discussions about the power and responsibility of artists to use their platform for social change and activism. It also raised questions about the boundaries of artistic expression and the role of the media in shaping public perceptions.

Despite the challenges she faced, Sinead O'Connor's protest ultimately left a lasting impact on the world. It served as a catalyst for discussions about systemic abuse and the need for accountability within religious institutions. Her willingness to confront uncomfortable truths resonated with many, inspiring others to use their voices to challenge injustice and advocate for change.

Time passed, perspectives on Sinead's protest began to shift. While the controversy remained a significant part of her legacy, her musical talents and unapologetic authenticity endured. She continued to release albums, exploring various musical styles and collaborating with artists across genres. With each release, she reaffirmed her status as a formidable musician and artist, proving that her protest did not define her entire career.

Her protest heard around the world remains a testament to the power of artistic expression and the courage to stand up for one's beliefs. It serves as a reminder that artists have a unique ability to provoke thought, challenge societal norms, and inspire change. As the world continues to grapple with issues of social justice and religious accountability, Sinead's act of defiance continues to resonate as a pivotal moment in the history of art and activism.

Chapter 4

Struggles and Triumphs

As Sinead O'Connor's career progressed, her personal life remained marked by a series of struggles and triumphs. Behind the curtain of her fame, she grappled with inner demons and emotional turmoil, facing challenges that tested her resilience and strength. This chapter delves into the highs and lows of Sinead's journey, revealing the complex interplay between her music, mental health, and pursuit of spiritual enlightenment.

Amidst the glitz and glamour of the music industry, Sinead battled with mental health issues that often threatened to overshadow

24

her achievements. Diagnosed with bipolar disorder, she experienced extreme mood swings that deeply affected her well-being and relationships. The burden of fame and the relentless media scrutiny only exacerbated her struggles, leading to periods of isolation and self-reflection.

In her quest for personal growth and understanding, Sinead embarked on a spiritual journey that took her through various paths and belief systems. Following her protest on "Saturday Night Live," she embraced Rastafarianism and changed her name to "Shuhada Davitt." Later, she converted to Islam, adopting the name "Magda Davitt." These transitions were reflective of her desire to find solace and meaning in a world that often felt overwhelming.

Throughout her career, Sinead's music remained a powerful outlet for her emotions and thoughts. Her albums, such as "I Do Not Want What I Haven't Got" and "Universal Mother," further showcased her songwriting prowess and emotional depth. The heart-wrenching ballad "**Nothing Compares 2 U**," a cover of Prince's song, became her most iconic and commercially successful hit, solidifying her status as a vocal powerhouse.

Despite the accolades and commercial success, Sinead's personal life was marked by a series of turbulent relationships and marriages. Her openness about her struggles with love and vulnerability endeared her to many, but it also exposed her to public scrutiny and criticism. Yet, through it all, Sinead remained unapologetically herself, a woman who wore her heart on her sleeve and refused to conform to societal expectations.

The years passed and Sinead continued to navigate the music industry with her characteristic defiance. However, she faced challenges in maintaining the same level of commercial success that she achieved in the early years of her career. The changing landscape of the music industry and her own battles with mental health contributed to this shift. Nevertheless, she persisted, always staying true to her artistic vision and artistic integrity.

Throughout her life, Sinead's advocacy for social and political causes never waned. She fearlessly spoke out against injustice, campaigned for LGBTQ+ rights, and fought for the rights of abuse survivors. Her humanitarian efforts demonstrated her unwavering commitment to using her platform for positive change, even amidst her own personal struggles.

In 2018, Sinead revealed that she had been struggling with suicidal thoughts for years. This public admission shed light on the ongoing stigma surrounding mental health, inspiring a new conversation about the importance of empathy and support for those battling emotional challenges.

In more recent years, Sinead embarked on a new chapter in her life, embracing a quieter existence and focusing on her mental and emotional well-being. She found solace in her faith and sought inner peace away from the public eye. Her journey continues to inspire others, as she remains an enduring symbol of resilience and artistic integrity.

As the chapter comes to a close, it becomes clear that Sinead O'Connor's legacy extends far beyond her musical achievements. Her struggles and triumphs have touched the lives of countless individuals, offering a glimmer of hope and a reminder that the human spirit can endure and overcome even in the face of adversity. Sinead O'Connor's story serves as a testament to the power of music, activism, and self-discovery, and her journey continues to resonate with audiences worldwide.

Chapter 5

Musical Evolution

Throughout her illustrious career, Sinead O'Connor's musical evolution was a testament to her artistic versatility and willingness to explore new frontiers. As she continued to push the boundaries of her artistry, she fearlessly ventured into diverse musical territories, captivating audiences with her emotive vocals and thought-provoking lyrics.

Following the commercial success of "The Lion and the Cobra," Sinead's second album, "*I Do Not Want What I Haven't Got,*" marked a pivotal moment in her musical journey. Released in 1990, the album featured the iconic hit "*Nothing Compares 2 U*," which catapulted her to global stardom. The song's heartrending performance, accompanied by the iconic music video featuring Sinead's tearful face, struck a chord with audiences worldwide, resonating with its raw and emotive power.

As the '90s progressed, Sinead goes deeper into exploring her musical identity. With each album, she fearlessly experimented with different genres, demonstrating her ability to infuse her distinctive vocals into diverse styles. "Am I Not Your Girl?" showcased her love for jazz standards, where she put her unique spin on classic songs from the likes of Ella Fitzgerald and Billie Holiday.

Not content with sticking to one musical path, Sinead continued her evolution with "Universal Mother" in 1994, where she embraced a more folk-influenced sound. The album's title track and "Red Football" revealed her ever-evolving songwriting talents and her ability to tackle deeply personal themes with unapologetic honesty.

In the late '90s and early 2000s, Sinead ventured into the world of reggae with "Throw Down Your Arms." The album featured covers of classic reggae songs, showcasing her versatility as an artist. Her passionate delivery and reverence for the genre won praise from fans and critics alike, solidifying her reputation as an artist willing to fearlessly reinterpret and breathe new life into beloved classics.

Throughout her musical evolution, Sinead's collaborations with other artists further enriched her body of work. She joined forces with artists like Peter Gabriel, Massive Attack, and The Edge, among others, infusing her unique vocal style into collaborative efforts that pushed artistic boundaries.

Sinead's ability to explore diverse musical genres was matched by her commitment to social and political activism. Her music often served as a platform to address pressing issues such as war, human rights, and environmental concerns. She continued to use her voice to advocate for change, blending her art with her convictions to create a powerful and impactful message.

As she entered the 2010s, Sinead's musical journey took yet another turn. Her album "How About I Be Me (And You Be You)?" marked a return to her singer-songwriter roots, delivering deeply personal and introspective songs that showcased her continued growth as an artist and a woman. The album's lead single, "The Wolf is Getting Married," garnered critical acclaim, signaling a renewed sense of creative energy.

In 2014, Sinead released "I'm Not Bossy, I'm the Boss," which further cemented her evolution as a genre-bending artist. This album delved into rock and pop influences, allowing Sinead to showcase her versatility once again. With tracks like "Take Me to Church" and "James Brown," she proved that her artistic fire was far from extinguished.

As the chapter on Sinead O'Connor's musical evolution draws to a close, it becomes evident that her career has been a remarkable journey of reinvention and growth. She defied categorization, remaining untethered to any specific genre or label. Instead, she embraced the freedom of artistic expression, constantly challenging herself and her audience to explore new sonic landscapes.

Her unwavering commitment to authenticity and her courage to tackle complex themes in her music have left an enduring impact on the music industry and the hearts of her devoted fans. Sinead O'Connor's musical evolution is a testament to the power of artistic exploration, self-discovery, and the unyielding spirit of a true artist. As she continues to defy expectations and transcend musical boundaries, her legacy as a pioneering and influential figure in the world of music remains unshakable.

Chapter 6

Love, Loss, and Redemption

In the midst of Sinead O'Connor's musical evolution, her personal life remained intertwined with a series of profound experiences that shaped her journey of love, loss, and redemption. As a woman who wore her heart on her sleeve, she navigated the complexities of relationships and motherhood while grappling with the impact of her tumultuous past.

Love had always been a driving force in Sinead's life. Her search for love and connection often played out in her music, where she bared her soul through heartfelt lyrics and emotionally charged performances. However, the quest for love was not without its challenges. Throughout her life, Sinead struggled to find lasting romantic relationships that could withstand the pressures of her career and the relentless media scrutiny.

Marriage, for Sinead, was a journey of hope and heartbreak. She wedded four times, with each union bringing its own set of joys and struggles. Her marriages to music producer John Reynolds, journalist Nicholas Sommerlad, musician Steve Cooney, and therapist Barry Herridge were marked by the complexities of love, passion, and personal growth. These experiences influenced her music and provided a canvas for her to express the joys and sorrows of intimate relationships.

Motherhood was another significant aspect of Sinead's life, and it brought profound joy and transformation. As a mother to four children, she embraced the role with love and devotion. However, the pressures of balancing a demanding career with motherhood proved to be a challenging tightrope to walk. Despite the hardships, Sinead cherished her role as a mother and drew strength from her children in her darkest moments.

Yet, amidst the love and joy, loss also visited Sinead's life, leaving a deep impact on her spirit. The death of her beloved mother, Marie, in a car accident in 1985, shook her to the core and intensified the emotional turmoil she carried from her troubled childhood. Grief became a constant companion, shaping her perspectives on life and mortality, and inspiring songs like "Fire on Babylon" that channeled her pain into art.

As her continued to flourish, so did her battle with mental health. The emotional toll of her past, coupled with the pressures of fame and the challenges of personal relationships, led her to grapple with depression and anxiety. Her candidness about her struggles shattered the stigma surrounding mental health in the public eye, inspiring empathy and understanding from her fans.

In the face of adversity, redemption and spiritual awakening became guiding lights in Sinead's life. Her quest for spiritual enlightenment took her through different belief systems, ultimately leading her to embrace Islam and change her name to "*Magda Davitt*." Faith provided her with a sense of purpose, grounding her as she navigated life's storms.

In the wake of personal challenges, Sinead sought redemption through her music and her advocacy work. She used her platform to champion social causes, standing up for the rights of marginalized communities, and speaking out against injustice. Her passionate commitment to human rights and activism endeared her to many and solidified her legacy as more than just a musician but also as an agent of positive change.

As the chapter unfolds, the duality of Sinead O'Connor's life becomes evident—the intertwining of love and loss, pain and redemption. Her unwavering authenticity and vulnerability in her music and her personal life endeared her to a devoted fan base who saw in her a reflection of their own struggles and triumphs.

In recent years, Sinead embraced a quieter existence, focusing on her mental and emotional well-being. She retreated from the public eye, seeking refuge in her faith and her family. Her journey of love, loss, and redemption continues, leaving an indelible mark on the world and inspiring generations to come.

As the chapter draws to a close, it becomes clear that Sinead O'Connor's life is a tapestry of profound experiences, woven together with the threads of love, pain, and a relentless quest for self-discovery. Her journey serves as a testament to the resilience of the human spirit and the redemptive power of music, love, and personal growth. Sinead's legacy remains alive through her music, activism, and the impact she has left on the hearts of those who have been touched by her art and her spirit.

Chapter 7

Legacy and Influence

Sinead O'Connor's legacy as a pioneering artist and cultural icon extends far beyond her commercial success and critical acclaim. Her impact on the music industry and society at large is a testament to the power of authenticity, fearlessness, and unapologetic self-expression. As her journey unfolded, Sinead left an indelible mark on the hearts and minds of millions worldwide, forever influencing the landscape of music, activism, and social consciousness.

One of Sinead's most significant contributions to music was her unique vocal style and emotive delivery. Her haunting voice possessed a raw power that could convey a myriad of emotions, from vulnerability and sorrow to defiance and strength. Her ability to infuse her songs with raw emotion allowed listeners to connect with her on a deeply personal level, creating a profound and lasting impact on the hearts of her fans.

Beyond her vocal talent, Sinead's songwriting was equally transformative. Her lyrics delved into themes of love, loss, spirituality, and social justice with unyielding honesty. She was unafraid to tackle difficult subjects, using her music as a platform to shed light on the injustices of the world and to advocate for positive change. Her songs resonated with audiences, inspiring empathy and understanding, and empowering listeners to confront their own emotions and beliefs.

Sinead's cultural impact also extended to her advocacy work. Throughout her career, she fearlessly spoke out against injustice and stood up for the rights of marginalized communities. From her public protests and political statements to her charitable endeavors, she used her platform to amplify the voices of the oppressed and to champion human rights causes. Her commitment to activism not only inspired her fans but also paved the way for a new generation of socially conscious artists.

Her boldness and authenticity made her a trailblazer for women in the music industry.

Sinead shattered gender norms and defied expectations, rejecting the confines of traditional femininity and embracing a distinctive androgynous appearance. Her refusal to conform to societal norms challenged perceptions of female artists, paving the way for greater acceptance of diverse gender expressions in the entertainment world.

Moreover, her willingness to confront mental health issues head-on had a profound impact on public perception and the discourse surrounding mental health. By candidly discussing her struggles with depression and anxiety, she humanized these challenges and helped break down the stigma associated with mental health. Her openness inspired others to seek help and support, fostering a more compassionate and empathetic understanding of mental health issues.

Sinead's impact on future generations of musicians is undeniable. Her fearless exploration of different musical styles and her boundary-pushing approach to artistry inspired countless artists to embrace their own creativity without fear of judgment. She proved that music could be a vehicle for self-expression and a platform for social change, leaving a profound influence on the world of music and activism.

The enduring relevance of Sinead O'Connor's music and message can be seen in the tributes and homages paid to her by other artists. Her cover of Prince's "Nothing

Compares 2 U" became an iconic rendition that resonated with audiences globally. Many artists have cited her as a significant influence on their careers, demonstrating the far-reaching impact of her artistry and authenticity.

As the chapter on Sinead O'Connor's legacy and influence draws to a close, it becomes evident that her impact on the world of music and beyond is immeasurable. Her authenticity, courage, and unyielding commitment to her beliefs have left an indelible mark on society. Through her music and advocacy, she continues to inspire change and encourage others to fearlessly express their truth. Sinead O'Connor's legacy stands as a testament to the transformative power of art, the importance of using one's voice for positive change, and the enduring spirit of a true rebel with a cause.

Death and Funeral

How did Sinéad O'Connor die?

On the day the news broke, no cause of death was given. The Guardian reported that London Metropolitan Police were called at 11.18 am Wednesday morning to an "unresponsive woman" at a residential address in south London. O'Connor had moved to the city just weeks prior to her death. "Officers attended. A 56-year-old woman was pronounced dead at the scene. Next of kin have been notified. The death is not being treated as suspicious. A file will be prepared for the coroner."

The Irish Times was the first outlet to report that O'Connor had passed, with a statement from her family that read: "It is with great sadness that we announce the passing of our beloved Sinéad. Her family and friends are devastated and have requested privacy at this very difficult time."

Funeral

On August 8, 2023, Sinéad O'Connor was laid to rest in the coastal town of Bray, south of Dublin, Ireland. O'Connor, who converted to Islam in 2018, had a funeral that reflected her faith and kept with an old Irish custom, as her coffin was first carried past her last family home. Prior to the procession, O'Connor's family held a private funeral service , according to RTE, which reported that Irish President Michael D. Higgins and

Taoiseach Leo Varadkar were in attendance as well as Bob Geldof and U2's frontman Bono were among the mourners

"The more she sang and spoke about her own pain, as well as about the pervasive sins in society that she witnessed, the more her voice and her words resonated with listeners and touched their hearts," Islamic scholar Umar Al-Qadri, who led the burial. He continued that she had been "gifted with a voice that moved a generation of young people" and "could reduce listeners to tears by her otherworldly resonance."

Conclusion

In this compelling biography book, we've journeyed through the remarkable life of Sinead O'Connor, a true rebel heart whose legacy extends far beyond her status as a music icon. From her troubled upbringing in Dublin, Ireland, to her meteoric rise to stardom and the controversies that defined her career, Sinead's story is one of resilience, authenticity, and unapologetic self-expression.

Throughout her musical evolution, Sinead fearlessly pushed the boundaries of artistry, exploring diverse genres and using her emotive voice to convey a profound range of emotions. Her songs became anthems of vulnerability and strength, touching the hearts of millions and leaving an enduring impact on the world of music.

Beyond her musical prowess, Sinead's advocacy work and willingness to use her platform for social and political causes set her apart as an artist with a powerful voice for change. She challenged norms, confronted injustices, and became a symbol of courage for those seeking to stand up against oppression and inequality.

Her journey was not without its struggles—battles with mental health, personal relationships, and the relentless pressures of fame all tested her spirit. Yet, Sinead's honesty about her own vulnerabilities shattered the stigma surrounding mental health and inspired a new era of compassion and understanding.

As we conclude this biography, it becomes evident that Sinead O'Connor's legacy is one that transcends time. Her impact on music, activism, and the world at large is an enduring testament to the transformative power of art and the unwavering commitment to truth. Her music will continue to inspire future generations of artists, and her fearless pursuit of justice and authenticity will serve as a guiding light for those seeking to make a difference in the world.

Sinead O'Connor's story is a tapestry of love, loss, redemption, and resilience—a narrative that resonates deeply with the human experience. As we bid farewell to this captivating journey, let us remember the rebel heart who dared to challenge conventions, speak her truth, and use her voice to create a more compassionate and just world. Her legacy lives on in the hearts of her devoted fans and in the profound impact she has left on the music industry, the realm of activism, and the hearts of millions around the globe.